Perceptions

The truth is just a perception

Shmilona Jain

Made with ❤ on the BookLeaf Publishing Platform
www.bookleafpub.in
www.bookleafpub.com

Dedication

To my family
And friends who became family
And family who became friends
To pieces of my heart that I have lost
You live in my poems....

Preface

I have been writing poetry since I was very young. I think I had many thoughts in my head and at that time, not many channels of communication were available. I used to send my poems to various competitions, and wrote in the school and college magazine. But more than that, during the time when I was a teenager , I used to write poems as a way of journaling my thoughts and emotions. Then, as the availability of the world wide web increased, I started writing a blog and then on social media. So I think writing poetry comes naturally to me. I find it easier to express in poetry than in prose.
A lot of friends and family members, have suggested I publish my poems. So when this opportunity came along, I thought of giving it a shot. So my poems depend on my mood. Some might be negative, some supremely positive and some are simply my perceptions of the world outside.
You might not like or enjoy all of them, but as I said, I am doing this for the people who told me, when I was very young, that there is a poet in me.

Acknowledgements

I thank Bookleaf publishing for providing me with this
opportunity to express.
I thank my family members for bearing with me and my
ways
I thank each and every person, that I have met and
interacted with in my life. Somewhere, somehow, you
are a part of my poems.

1 . Faces

Every face that I see
Somehow talks to me
They tell me stories
I haven't heard before
With every expression
I yearn for more.

The eyes! Oh, the eyes!
Intense and deep
The deepest and darkest secrets they keep.
And yet, when you hold them
In a direct, non-judgmental gaze
You unlock every box, you cross every maze.

And then my focus goes on the smile
Wry and wicked
Or innocent or guile
It makes the hero, a villian
The villian, the cause
The cause for every event

Worth criticism or applause.

The lines, the curves
Long and deep
Hold moments that turned
Into memories, to keep.

And so every face
Has a story to tell
It doesn't come as a whisper
or a loud yell
Its there for me to read,
to experience and to see
In a face that turns
to look at me.

2. Can you tell time?

Can you tell time?
Because I cannot
The numbers and the colon
Is all that I have got
But is it just a number?
That is displayed on my clock
Or is there something more
To all the time that I have got?
What is the essence of the moment?
When it says it's 12 o'clock
What controls that moment?
Before the needles take a walk.
Who knows what will happen ?
With every step that I take
In which moment will I win?
Which moment will I not make?
I may try my hardest
To predict what happens next
To design the next moment
Write the details of every text.

But the truth is that these seconds
That simply pass by
Truly control me
And I don't know the reason why
I may be able to affect it
But I don't control my time
It's really something else
That is making these designs.
So can you tell time?
I most certainly cannot.
The numbers and the colon
Is truly all that I've got.

3. The girl without the masks

Nature has a way of bringing me out
Of removing all the masks
I can truly do without
The masks that the days add on my face
As I go through life
Running every race

And then I walk into my garden
And water the plants
And every new leaf
Makes me want to dance
Every new bud
Fills me with hope
Of a flower, unborn
And yet it stirs,
it evokes
The me without the lies
The me before the cries
The me before the tasks

The me without the masks

It feels as if the flower
Is blossoming within me
And opening all windows
For the sun to come and see
That girl who twirled
Barefoot on the grass
Who opened her hair
And let the wind pass
Unafraid of how she looks
In their eyes
Carefree of the words
Comments and despise
That girl without the masks
The garments and the gems
That girl true in form
Without any amends

And that is why nature calls to me
It's true
It's you
Without purpose
Or duty
Without intent
Or extent
Without vies

Or lies
It's simple, it's raw
Just what meets the eyes.

4. Comfortably Dumb

I have a lot to say but I don't
I want to start a battle but I wont
What's the point of having a say?
When you can't use it everyday
The damage that's done won't go
And the path to recovery is slow
But I am learning everyday
To hold my breath
From coming out the wrong way
From not following my heart, but rules
To tinker and play with their tools
I am learning to not express
To not deliver or impress
I am growing everyday
Layers of metal around by clay
To bound the thoughts that run free
I stop my heart from being me

'Coz I have realized there is no need
To raise and nurture enemies

Live and let live
This is what it means
Don't talk
No one is listening to me
Be quiet and reserved in your ways
Sail silently through everyday
Its easy, when you don't feel and be numb
Its convenient to be comfortably dumb.

5. Demons

I have many demons
That I birthed in my life
From moments when I succumbed
To circumstances and their plights
And slowly as time went by
And I got on with my days
I forgot about these monsters
I had created on my way

But what is done is done
And what is born, remains
Even if you leave them
The demons don't go away

They are stronger than good hearts
They don't need your love and care
You might have left them in your past
But they take away their share

And you never notice

These shadows walking behind
But they are there, hiding and slithering
Out of sight and out of mind

And one day when you slow down
Or falter on your way
They stand up and overpower
Your wisdom and your say

And you try really hard
To get up and scare them away
They might scuttle and hide again
And make you think you have seized the day

But the truth is they didn't die
They simple quietened down
They learn that you gain strength
And won't crumble under their crown.
And you learn to not be afraid
To put a lock on their den
You can never defeat your demons
You learn to live above them

6. सिर्फ मैं क्यों बदलूं?

कभी थे उसकी शीतलता के चर्चे।
शर्माना उसका श्रृंगार था।
कोमलता उसकी खूबी थी।
खामोशी उसका गहना था।
फिर बोला गया, ऐ स्त्री तुम जागो।
तुम पुरुष से कम नहीं।
पढ़ो लिखो और आगे बढ़ो।
तुम्हारे बिना हम नही।
फिर बोला तुम काम करो, पर रहो ज़रा खबरदार।
क्योंकि तुम तो आगे बढ़ गई, पर पुरुष की सोच हो गई बेकार।
अब कहते हैं, तुम लड़ना सीखो।
अपना बचाव कर पाओ।
ये दुनिया बड़ी खराब है।
आगे बढ़ो पर अपना शास्त्र भी उठाओ।

इस पूरी कहानी में हमने सिर्फ स्त्री को बोला।
उठ, बदल, संभल कर चल।
कभी किसी ने ये नही बोला-
पुरुष संभल, होशियार बन।
सम्मान दे, हाथ पकड़।

वो भी तेरे जैसी है।
न कम, न ज्यादा, तेरे समान है वो।
तो जब वो बदले तो तू भी बदल।
चल अब उसके साथ चल।

7. I forgot

Things that you forget
Things that you forget and regret
Things that you shouldn't forget
And yet you forget
And thus regret

Things that you had decided are important
Things you kept carefully inside
They somehow manage to slip away
When you bring in a new thought in your mind

Why do thoughts just disappear?
Slip away and the mind is clear
Like they had never appeared
Like a light that disappears in a nightmare

Things that you want should stay
Tend to always slip away
And what remains are unimportant and random strays
Like how many times I sneezed yesterday.

Maybe what we hold near
We hold with a fear
'Coz we think we cannot bear
If they will disappear
And its the fear that takes them away
Not the love we gave it today
So if I once held a thought
Quite close to my heart
Its quite possible that in my wrought
Today, I simply forgot!

8. Dear Friend

Who is a friend I ask?
Someone who is there for every task?
Someone with whom I don't wear a mask.
Someone who answers before I ask.

Someone I may not meet everyday
Or speak to or think of all the time today
But when I read their name somewhere
If makes me smile
It fills my heart with warmth
And pause for a while

Someone I may not agree with all the time
Someone who annoys me once in a while
Yet I know that they will always be by my side
When I call them to hold my hand in a ride

Someone I look forward to seeing everyday
Who makes me bare my soul in everything I say

Someone who I know will be there till the end,
My smile begins with you my dear friend!

17

9. The sea

As I sit to write
An ode to the sea
A can smell the air
and feel the sand beneath me

Its quite surreal
The feeling I get
When I stare at the water
Its vastness, its depth

Its vastness makes you feel small
Like a speck in eternity
And its depth
makes you feel shallow
Your deepest thoughts, a triviality

And as you start to feel minute
Insignificant in front of magnanimity
A gentle wave touches your feet
And makes you feel a solidarity

With this grand and enchanting creation
The beginning of life and its every solution
It doesn't mock you for your ignorance
It doesn't reject you for your flaws
It accepts you as a wild moment
Which exists only for a pause.

O great sea!
I bow down to thee
To your vastness,
Beyond infinity
I am merely a flicker in time
A moment insignificant, a dime
And yet you touch my soul
And make me a part of your whole.

O great sea!
I bow down to thee
You give my insignificance
An individuality.

10. एक सिक्के के दो पहलू

एक सिक्के के दो पहलू, एक मैं और एक तू
एक सर है
दूसरा पूंछ
एक अंत है
तो एक कूच
एक साथ हैं दोनों हमेशा
मिलकर बनाते हैं एक इकाई
फिर भी देखे न एक दुसरे को
जैसे दो छोर के दो सिपाही
साथ है तो ही अर्थ है
अकेले जीवन व्यर्थ है
पर साथ देखने में असमर्थ है

एक उत्तर देखे
दूजा दक्षिण
ना मिले कभी पलछिन
और इसी द्वैत में है एक व्यक्तित्वा
एक परिभाषा, एक अस्तित्व

एक सिक्के के दो पहलू, एक मैं और एक तू

साथ हो कर भी देख ना पाते
एक दुसरे की आरज़ू

21

11. The mountains

The mountains call to me
Challenge me to climb
They smile as I step
Gently on the incline

I respect them as I tread
Gradually up their rise
Every step is of gratitude
For allowing me to abide
By their rules and their ways
Listening to what the wind says
Watching every stone and pebble
At all turns and bevels

As I rise high
I feel proud
That I managed to touch the cloud
But then I pause and catch my breath
And realize what it took instead
The climb took a little of me away

Took some sweat, some breath
some pride and some dismay
Made me stronger and purer
And happier within
Cooled my mind
And burnt my skin
Made me feel light
like the breeze
that runs along my skin
The strength of the sun
Moulds the metal within
The trees and the creatures
Smile at me
Welcoming me to their abode
Become a part of my history

The mountains call to me
And challenge me to climb
And I smile and take them on
Like a friend takes a jibe

12. Two words...that's all

A poem
A song
A wish
so long

A story
of glory
A battle
a victory

A rise
and a fall
then again
stand tall

Give up
or give it all
and then
just stall

Two words
That's all!

25

13. Children

Children
just what, do we write about them
They teach you
They beseech you
To listen to them

Their thoughts
Their ideas
So new and pure
There is so much to learn
From their methods and cure

Their ways are new,
unmatched, without review
And so they are
unlearnt and true

The smile
That stays a while
melts the hardest metal

stops the fastest ride

Their hugs
Godsent!
With so much love
Can heal every wound
whether deep or up above

And so I just laugh
and play with them
They give me more
Than I can ever give them.

14. Morning sun

The morning sun
Waking up with me
In a blanket of clouds
Trying to break free
To unleash it's power
And charge up the day
And fill us with the warmth
Of every morning ray

But right now, like me
It's trying to leave it's bed
Leave the cozy blanket
And rise up instead

It's soft and orange
And smiling at me
Telling me, 'Get up
Let's start the day and be free.
If comfort and safety
Let's take some challenges today

And shine bright at every place
No matter what they say.'

The morning sun,
It talks to me
We bring in the day together
Smiling and free

15. Fly like an eagle

Fly like an eagle
Soar in the sky
Look down at the world
And smile and go by

Flap your wings to rise above
And then just leave them open and be free
If you aren't scared of the fall
You glide confidently

The other birds may talk
But they are scared of these
So you maintain your poise
And dignity

So fly like an eagle
Fly high in the sky
Be alone and content
And they will never know why

16. When you hold my gaze

That moment when you hold my gaze
We talk without words
And work through the maze
Of each other's minds
And each other's days
And smile at the fact
That we can converse this way

I know what you are thinking
How you feel inside
You know all my secrets
Whispered across a mile

When you hold my gaze
You hold me in your arms
Your smile from a distance
Has incredible charm
It feels like a hug
Like a gift from up above

Like life is just you and me
Forever and eternity

17. Summer

Summer for some
Is pleasant and nice
The warmth of the sun
Melts the ice

The breeze is warm
As it touches the skin
No chills, no sniffles
Such pleasant weather thrills

Go out on the beach
and enjoy the water
and let the sun work
its way on your matter

They pleasant times
To go out and play
The day is longer and here to stay

Summer for some

Is hotter than the oven
The breeze also heats up
and the sun is brazen

Its better to avoid
stay in all day
And drink enough water
To calm the dismay

Going out is a task
Taken up by heroes
Who are brave enough to
beat the heat
and sweat it out on the street
The others just stay home
And pray for the rain
To calm the earth down
Its burn and its pain

Summer means so much
On both the sides
But the feeling is different
Some fear, some nice.

18. Sunsets

Sunsets
And how they paint the sky
The colour palette magnificent
And unique and exemplified

The artist
so great, perfect at his hues
mixes the colours
and creates magic in the views

With strokes of orange, pink, and gold,
A story whispered, soft yet bold,
Each canvas stretches far and wide,
And everyday a new painting meets our eyes.

Clouds aflame with passion's glow,
A fleeting moment, time moves slow,
Their borders are etched in silver lines
adding detail to this grandeur vague yet fine

And then as if this wasn't all
He adds a few birds
at random points small
Yet so precise is their movement
That they simply add charm
To this glorious display
Above us all

Sunsets
I look forward to everyday
It's nature's supremacy
On display

19. On the road

On the road
behind my wheels
steering through life
and its turns and bends

I hum a tune
unknown to me
maybe something
that my mind wends

I catch a smile
on my lips
for no reason
or rhyme

Don't know who
I am smiling at
There's no one with me
this time

It feels good
to be able to hold
The road with the wheels
Under my control

It feels like
something belongs to me
this road
this moment
this wheel.

20. The run before the sun

A run at dawn
Before the sun comes on
Feels so good
Like a beginning strong

The smiles at others
Walking past you
Like celebrating the fact
That the sun is still due

Those early birds,
Chirp on the trees
Waking each other up
To start the day with me

The dog's on their way
To their homes and beds
Look at you with disdain
'Why don't you go home instead?'

The light morning breeze
Wet with dew
Moistens your skin
Caressing you

And then slowly
Like the blanket just removed
The first few rays
Come out to touch you

And you look at the sun and smile
'Get up my dear! Its time.'
I am all charged up to start the day
Bring on the light and all you have to say!

21. A letter never sent

Once upon a time
I wrote a letter in rhyme
I poured my heart to you
All things that I wanted to do

I let the pen take control
And across the paper stroll
While my mind just guided the way
With words that came its way

I wrote without thought or caution
Everything from prizes to emotion
I wrote about every kind
Of ramblings in my mind

And when the paper came to an end
I signed it, 'From your friend.'
I folded it neatly with a smile
And placed it in the envelope in style

With love I wrote your name
And sealed it just the same
Then got up to post it to you
And then stopped in a step or two

I was suddenly filled with doubt
What would you think about
Me when you get the mail
Would I succeed or would I fail
In transferring my thoughts to you
What would it mean to you?

And the thoughts filled me with fear
of losing a friend so dear
And so instead of posting it to you
The letter went into subdue

Its still hiding in my cupboard
Lost in time
A letter I wrote
To a friend of mine.

www.ingramcontent.com/pod-product-compliance
Lightning Source LLC
LaVergne TN
LVHW021303200726
843509LV00012B/1764